To

Wanda my best
friend

From

Ruth

Happy 57th Birthday!!
3/20/04

365 Day Brighteners™ for a Treasured Friend
© 2003 DaySpring Cards, Inc.
Published by Garborg's™, a brand of DaySpring Cards, Inc.
Siloam Springs, Arkansas

Scripture quotations are from the following sources: The HOLY BIBLE, NEW INTERNATIONAL VERSION® (NIV)® © 1973, 1978, 1984 by International Bible Society. Used by permission of Zondervan Publishing House. THE MESSAGE © Eugene H. Peterson 1993, 1994, 1995. Used by permission of NavPress Publishing Group. All rights reserved. The Living Bible (TLB) © 1971 by permission of Tyndale House Publishers, Inc., Wheaton, IL. The New Revised Standard Version of the Bible (NRSV) © 1989 Division of Christian Education, National Council of Churches. Used by permission of Zondervan Publishing House.

ISBN 1-58061-575-9   Printed In China

365 DAY BRIGHTENERS

for a
Treasured
Friend

GARBORG'S
because an everyday by a gift

365 DAY BRIGHTENERS

for a Treasured Friend

Life begins each morning.... Each morning is the open door to a new world—new vistas, new aims, new tryings.

Leigh Hodges

January 1

Every day under the sun is a gift. Receive it with eagerness. Treat it kindly. Share it with joy. Each night return it to the Giver who will make it bright and shiny again before the next sunrise.

Friends are of utmost importance. We love, trust, get hurt, sometimes get mad, but we love and trust anyhow, because that's the best way to let our friendship grow.

January 3

January 4

If I knew you and you knew me,
If both of us could clearly see,
And with an inner sight divine
The meaning of your heart and mine,
I'm sure that we would differ less,
And clasp our hands in friendliness;
Our thoughts would pleasantly agree
If I knew you and you knew me.

Nixon Waterman

Friendship is one of the sweetest joys of life.

Charles H. Spurgeon

Be truly glad! There is wonderful joy ahead.

1 Peter 1:6 TLB

January 5

January 6

Live as though you believe that the power behind the universe is a power of love, a personal power of love, a love so great that all of us really do matter to Him.

Madeleine L'Engle

$\mathcal{D}$on't ever let yourself get so busy that you miss those little but important extras in life—the beauty of a day...the smile of a friend...the serenity of a quiet moment alone. For it is often life's smallest pleasures and gentlest joys that make the biggest and most lasting difference.

$\mathcal{J}$anuary 7

January 8

Hand
Grasps hand, eye lights eye in good
friendship,
And great hearts expand,
And grow one in the sense of this world's life.

Robert Browning

Living is the constant adjustment of thought to life and life to thought in such a way that we are always growing, always experiencing new things in the old and old things in the new.

Thomas Merton

January 9

January 10

Take delight in the Lord,
and he will give you the desires of your heart.

Psalm 37:4 NRSV

$\mathcal{A}$ friend is able to see you as the
wonderful person God created you to be.

Ann D. Parrish

$\mathcal{J}$anuary 11

January 12

Life is so full of meaning and purpose, so full of beauty—beneath its covering—that you will find that earth but cloaks your heaven.

Fra Giovanni

What we do does not give us simplicity,
but it does put us in the place where we
can receive it. It sets our lives before God
in such a way that He can work into us the
grace of simplicity.

Richard J. Foster

January 13

January 14

There's a miracle called friendship
That dwells within the heart,
And you don't know how it happens
Or where it gets its start.
But the happiness it brings you
Always gives a special lift,
And you realize that friendship
Is life's most precious gift.

Look to the Lord and his strength;
seek his face always.
Remember the wonders he has done.

Psalm 105:4-5 NIV

January 15

January 16

True contentment is a real, even an active, virtue—not only affirmative but creative. It is the power of getting out of any situation all there is in it.

G. K. Chesterton

I see in the stars, in the rivers, I see in the open fields, patches of heaven and threads of paradise. Let me sew the earth, the day, the way of my life into a pattern that forms a quilt, God's quilt, to keep me warm today and always.

Christopher de Vinck

January 17

January 18

Long years you've kept the door ajar
To greet me, coming from afar:
Long years in my accustomed place
I've read my welcome in your face.

Robert Bridges

Friends find the sweetest sense of
happiness comes from simply being together.

January 19

January 20

You are joined together with peace through the Spirit, so make every effort to continue together in this way.

Ephesians 4:3 NCV

There are times when encouragement
means such a lot. And a word is
enough to convey it.

Grace Stricker Dawson

January 21

January 22

Blessed are the ones God sends to show
His love for us...our friends.

If peace be in the heart the wildest winter storm is full of solemn beauty.

C. F. Richardson

January 23

January 24

The fountain of beauty is the heart, and every generous thought illustrates the walls of your chamber.

Francis Quarles

May the Lord continually bless you with heaven's blessings as well as with human joys.

Psalm 128:5 TLB

January 25

January 26

I cannot count the number of times I have been strengthened by another woman's heartfelt hug, appreciative note, surprise gift, or caring questions...my friends are an oasis to me, encouraging me to go on. They are essential to my well-being.

Dee Brestin

$\mathcal{G}$od bless the friend who sees my needs
and reaches out a hand,
who lifts me up, who prays for me,
and helps me understand.

Amanda Bradley

$\mathcal{J}$anuary 27

January 28

God is all that is good, as I see it—and the goodness that all things have, it is He.

Julian of Norwich

$\mathcal{C}$elebration is more than a happy
feeling. Celebration is an experience.
It is liking others, accepting others,
laughing with others.

Douglas R. Stuva

$\mathcal{J}$anuary 29

January 30

Friendship is holding hands and
sticking together.

*There is a friend who sticks closer
than a brother.*

Proverbs 18:24 TLB

$\mathcal{G}$od has a wonderful plan for each person.... He knew even before He created this world what beauty He would bring forth from our lives.

Louis B. Wyly

$\mathcal{J}$anuary 31

February 1

Like branches on a tree we grow in different directions yet our roots remain as one. Each of our lives will always be a special part of the other.

There is an exquisite melody in every heart. If we listen closely, we can hear each other's song. A friend knows the song in your heart and responds with beautiful harmony.

February 2

February 3

Our brightest blazes of gladness are commonly kindled by unexpected sparks.

Samuel Johnson

He surrounds me with loving-kindness
and tender mercies. He fills my life
with good things!

Psalm 103:4-5 TLB

February 4

February 5

I breathed a song into the air;
It fell to earth, I know not where....
and the song, from beginning to end,
I found again in the heart of a friend.

Longfellow

The most universally awesome experience that mankind knows is to stand alone on a clear night and look at the stars. It was God who first set the stars in space; He is their Maker and Master.... Such are His power and His majesty.

J. I. Packer

February 6

February 7

Every morning is a fresh opportunity to find God's extraordinary joy in the most ordinary places.

Janet L. Weaver Smith

I have learned that to have a good friend is the purest of all God's gifts, for it is a love that has no exchange of payment.

Frances Farmer

February 8

February 9

God has given each of you some special
abilities; be sure to use them to help each
other, passing on to others God's
many kinds of blessings.

1 Peter 4:10 TLB

L ove is the master key that opens the
gates of happiness.

Oliver Wendell Holmes

F ebruary 10

February 11

My fondest hope is that I may be worthy of a place in your friendship, and being admitted to that sacred circle, that I may never prove unfaithful to your trust in me.

Edwin Osgood Grover

$\mathcal{A}$ joyful heart is like the sunshine of God's love, the hope of eternal happiness.

Mother Teresa

$\mathcal{F}$ebruary 12

February 13

The good for which we are born into this world is that we may learn to love.

George MacDonald

Kindness always blesses the heart of the giver. Whatever you do, do it with kindness and love.

1 Corinthians 16:14 TLB

February 14

February 15

No love, no friendship can cross the path
of our destiny without leaving some
mark on it forever.

François Mauriac

Simplicity means a return to the posture
of dependence. Like children we live in a
of trust. What we have we receive as a gift.

Richard J. Foster

February 16

February 17

And so, at this time,
I greet you.
Not quite as the world
sends greetings,
but with profound esteem
and with the prayer
that for you
now and forever,
the day breaks,
and the shadows flee away.

Fra Giovanni

I t isn't the big pleasures that count the
most; it's making a great deal out
of the little ones.

Jean Webster

February 18

February 19

The Lord is good to all,
and his compassion is over all that
he has made.

Psalm 145:9 NRSV

$\mathcal{A}$ true friend is one who is concerned about what we are becoming, who sees beyond the present relationship, and who cares deeply about us as a whole person.

Gloria Gaither

$\mathcal{F}$ebruary 20

February 21

Your greatest pleasure is that which rebounds from hearts that you have made glad.

Henry Ward Beecher

Good friends reveal themselves slowly, in the shimmer and shadow of living...in the years of shared experience.

February 22

February 23

The wonder of living is held within the beauty of silence, the glory of sunlight...the sweetness of fresh spring air, the quiet strength of earth, and the love that lies at the very root of all things.

Great is your love, reaching to the heavens; your faithfulness reaches to the skies.

Psalm 57:10 NIV

February 24

February 25

Love puts the fun in together...
the sad in apart...
the hope in tomorrow...
the joy in a heart.

What brings joy to the heart is not so much the friend's gifts as the friend's love.

Aelred of Rievaulx

February 26

February 27

Love is reaching, touching and caring, sharing sunshine and flowers, so many happy hours together.

Friends are angels who lift our feet when our own wings have trouble remembering how to fly.

February 28

February 29

May you be given more and more of God's kindness, peace, and love.

Jude 1:2 TLB

$\mathcal{A}$ friend is somebody who loves us with understanding, as well as emotion.

Robert Louis Stevenson

$\mathcal{M}$arch 1

I wished I had a box,
the biggest I could find,
I'd fill it right up to the brim
with everything that's kind....
Grateful words for joys received
I'd freely give away.
Oh, let us open wide a box
of praise for every day.

Friends...lift our spirits, keep us honest, stick with us when times are tough, and make mundane tasks enjoyable. No wonder we want to make friends.

Em Griffin

March 3

March 4

May your footsteps set you upon a lifetime journey of love. May you wake each day with His blessings and sleep each night in His keeping. And may you always walk in His tender care.

Friendship is a cadence of divine melody melting through the heart.

Mildmay

Love...binds everything together in perfect harmony.

Colossians 3:14 NRSV

March 5

March 6

Sometimes it is a slender thread,
Sometimes a strong, stout rope;
She clings to one end,
I the other;
She calls it friendship;
I call it hope.

Lois Wyse

That is God's call to us—simply to be people who are content to live close to Him and to renew the kind of life in which the closeness is felt and experienced.

Thomas Merton

March 7

March 8

The glory of friendship is found in the inspiration that comes when I discover that someone else believes in me and is willing to trust me with their friendship.

We all stumble, every one of us. That's why it's a comfort to go hand in hand.

Emily Kimbrough

March 9

March 10

Your friendship helps me get over the rough spots in life.

Carry each other's burdens.

Galatians 6:2 NIV

$\mathcal{Y}$ou are God's created beauty and the
focus of His affection and delight.

Janet L. Weaver Smith

$\mathcal{M}$arch 11

March 12

True friends are never far apart,
each keeps the other in her heart.

Life begets life. Energy creates energy. It is by spending oneself that one becomes rich.

Sarah Bernhardt

March 13

March 14

Eating lunch with a friend. Trying to do a decent day's work. Hearing the rain patter against the window. There is no event so commonplace but that God is present within it, always hiddenly, always leaving you room to recognize Him or not to recognize Him.

Frederich Buechner

When we obey him, every path he guides us on is fragrant with his loving-kindness and his truth.

Psalm 25:10 TLB

March 15

March 16

Friendship is the breathing rose, with sweets in every fold.

Oliver Wendell Holmes

Everything in life is most
fundamentally a gift. And you receive it best,
and you live it best, by holding it with
very open hands.

Leo O'Donovan

March 17

March 18

Some blessings—like rainbows after rain or a friend's listening ear—are extraordinary gifts waiting to be discovered in an ordinary day.

R̲ight now a moment of time is fleeting
by! Capture its reality.... Become
that moment.

Paul Cézanne

M̲arch 19

March 20

When we love each other God lives in us and his love within us grows ever stronger.

1 John 4:12 TLB

$\mathcal{Y}$ou're my friend—
What a thing friendship is,
world without end!

Robert Browning

$\mathcal{M}$arch 21

March 22

A true friend inspires you to believe the best in yourself, to keep pursuing your deepest dreams. Most wonderful of all, she celebrates all your successes as if they were her own!

If instead of a gem, or even a flower, we should cast the gift of a loving thought into the heart of a friend; that would be giving as the angels give.

George MacDonald

March 23

March 24

Every time you smile at someone, it is an
action of love, a gift to that person,
a beautiful thing.

Mother Teresa

If I rise on the wings of the dawn,
if I settle on the far side of the sea,
even there your hand will guide me,
your right hand will hold me fast.

Psalm 139:9-10 NIV

March 25

March 26

Keep your face to the sunshine and you
cannot see the shadows.

Helen Keller

$\mathcal{S}$o shall a friendship fill each heart
With perfume sweet as roses are,
That even though we be apart,
We'll scent the fragrance from afar.

Georgia McCoy

$\mathcal{M}$arch 27

March 28

Open your hearts to the love God instills.... God loves you tenderly. What He gives you is not to be kept under lock and key, but to be shared.

Mother Teresa

$\mathcal{F}$riends are an indispensable part of a meaningful life. They are the ones who share our burdens and multiply our blessings.

Beverly LaHaye

$\mathcal{M}$arch 29

March 30

Whatever is true, whatever is noble,
whatever is right, whatever is pure, whatever
is lovely, whatever is admirable—if anything is
excellent or praiseworthy—
think about such things.

Philippians 4:8 NIV

Friends find the sweetest sense of
happiness comes from simply being together.

March 31

Recall it as often as you wish, a happy memory never wears out.

Libbie Fudim

$\mathcal{A}$ good friend is a connection to life—a
tie to the past, a road to the future, the key
to sanity in a totally insane world.

Lois Wyse

$\mathcal{A}$pril 2

April 3

If we just give God the little that we have,
we can trust Him to make it go around.

Gloria Gaither

$\mathcal{L}$ove...always protects, always trusts,
always hopes, always perseveres.

1 Corinthians 13:6-7 NIV

$\mathcal{A}$pril 4

April 5

Jesus cannot forget us; we have been graven on the palms of His hands.

Lois Picillo

I count your friendship one of the chiefest pleasures of my life, a comfort in time of doubt and trouble, a joy in time of prosperity and success, and an inspiration at all times.

Edwin Osgood Grover

April 6

April 7

All the things in this world are gifts and signs of God's love to us. The whole world is a love letter from God.

Peter Kreeft

Blue skies with white clouds on summer days. A myriad of stars on clear moonlit nights. Tulips and roses and violets and dandelions and daisies. Bluebirds and laughter and sunshine and Easter. See how He loves us!

Alice Chapin

April 8

April 9

Be...full of sympathy toward
each other, loving one another with tender
hearts and humble minds.

1 Peter 3:8 TLB

I still find each day too short for all the thoughts I want to think, all the walks I want to take, all the books I want to read, and all the friends I want to see. The longer I live, the more my mind dwells upon the beauty and the wonder of the world.

John Burroughs

April 10

April 11

The joyful birds prolong the strain,
their song with every spring renewed;
the air we breathe, and falling rain,
each softly whispers: God is good.

John Hampden Gurney

$\mathcal{A}$ loyal friend is like a safe shelter; find one, and you have found a treasure.

Sirach

$\mathcal{A}$pril 12

April 13

Were there no God we would be in this glorious world with grateful hearts and no one to thank.

Christina Rossetti

$\mathcal{S}$ay only what is good and helpful to those you are talking to, and what will give them a blessing.

Ephesians 4:29 TLB

$\mathcal{A}$pril 14

April 15

When we look for the good in others,
we discover the best in ourselves.

Martin Walsh

Friends help us feel secure. Our footing is surer when we know that someone accepts us as we are, someone has our best interests at heart, someone is always glad to see us, someone plans to stick around. There are few blessings like the blessing of a friend.

Emily Barnes and Donna Otto

April 16

Joy is the echo of God's life within us.

Joseph Marmion

$\mathcal{G}$ood friends are like stars.... You don't always see them, but you know they are always there.

$\mathcal{A}$pril 18

April 19

You give [us] drink from your river of delights. For with you is the fountain of life; in your light we see light.

Psalm 36:8-9 NIV

Life is short and we never have enough time for gladdening the hearts of those who travel the way with us. O, be swift to love! Make haste to be kind.

Henri Frédéric Amiel

April 20

April 21

May God send His love like sunshine in
His warm and gentle way,
To fill each corner of your heart
each moment of today.

I live for those who love me,
Whose hearts are kind and true,
For the human ties that bind me,
For the task by God assigned me,
For the bright hopes left behind me,
And the good that I can do.

George L. Banks

April 22

April 23

Allow your dreams a place in your prayers and plans. God-given dreams can help you move into the future He is preparing for you.

Barbara Johnson

The right word at the right time
is like a custom-made piece of jewelry,
and a wise friend's timely reprimand
is like a gold ring slipped on your finger.

Proverbs 25:11-12 THE MESSAGE

April 24

April 25

Whatever one possesses becomes of double value when we have the opportunity of sharing it with others.

Bouilly

$\mathcal{T}$o have a friend is to have one of the sweetest gifts that life can bring; to be a friend is to have a solemn and tender education of soul from day to day.

Amy Robertson Brown

$\mathcal{A}$pril 26

You have a unique message to deliver, a unique song to sing, a unique act of love to bestow. This message, this song, and this act of love have been entrusted exclusively to the one and only you.

John Powell

The most beautiful discovery true friends make is that they can grow separately without growing apart.

Elisabeth Foley

April 28

April 29

Each day can be the beginning of a wonderful future.

We know that in all things God works for the good of those who love him.

Romans 8:28 NIV

$\mathcal{F}$riendship is a sheltering tree;
Oh, the joys that come down shower-like!

Samuel Taylor Coleridge

$\mathcal{A}$pril 30

May 1

Love is the true means by which the world is enjoyed: our love to others, and others' love to us.

Thomas Traherne

$\mathcal{A}$ll the flowers God has made are beautiful. The rose in its glory and the lily in its whiteness do not rob the tiny violet of its sweet smell, or the daisy of its charming simplicity.

Thérèse of Lisieux

$\mathcal{M}$ay 2

May 3

The steadfast love of the Lord
never ceases, his mercies never
come to an end;
they are new every morning;
great is your faithfulness.

Lamentations 3:22-23 NRSV

God moves in a mysterious way
His wonders to perform;
He plants His footsteps on the sea,
And rides upon the storm.

William Cowper

May 4

May 5

It is the purest sign that we love someone if we choose to spend time idly in their presence when we could be doing something more constructive.

S. Cassidy

When you least expect it, a common thread—golden, at that—begins to weave together the fabric of friendship.

Mary Kay Shanley

May 7

Some people are so special that once they enter your life, it becomes richer and fuller and more wonderful than you ever thought it could be.

$\mathcal{Y}$ou are special and loved by the
One who created you.

*The Lord who created you...says..."I have called
you by name; you are mine."*

Isaiah 43:1 TLB

$\mathcal{M}$ay 8

May 9

It is a good and safe rule to sojourn in every place as if you meant to spend your life there, never omitting an opportunity of doing a kindness, or speaking a true word, or making a friend.

John Ruskin

In sunshine and in sorrow, we look for those who will always stand with us.

Lois Wyse

May 10

May 11

Her heart is like her garden,
Old-fashioned, quaint and sweet.
With here a wealth of blossoms,
And there a still retreat.

Alice E. Allen

When I look at the galaxies on a clear
night—when I look at the incredible brilliance
of creation, and think that this is what God is
like, then instead of feeling intimidated and
diminished by it, I am enlarged—I rejoice
that I am part of it.

Madeleine L'Engle

May 12

Happiness comes to those who are fair to others and are always just and good.

Psalm 106:3 TLB

$\mathcal{A}$ friend is a precious possession
Whose value increases with the years.
Someone who doesn't forsake us
when a difficult moment appears.

Henry Van Dyke

$\mathcal{M}$ay 14

May 15

One cannot collect all the beautiful shells on the beach. One can collect only a few, and they are more beautiful if they are few.

Anne Morrow Lindbergh

[L ove] is the divine vitality that every-where produces and restores life. To each and every one of us, it gives the power of working miracles if we will.

Lydia Maria Child

May 16

May 17

Though I have seen the oceans and mountains, though I have read great books and seen great works of art, though I have heard symphonies and tasted the best...foods, there is nothing greater or more beautiful than those people I love.

Christopher de Vinck

$\mathcal{T}$hank you for the treasure of your friendship...for showing me God's special heart of love.

Encourage each other to build each other up.

1 Thessalonians 5:11 TLB

$\mathcal{M}$ay 18

May 19

Friendship is a gift from God
that's blessed in every part...
born through love and loyalty...
conceived within the heart.

How necessary it is to cultivate a spirit of joy. To act lovingly is to begin to feel loving, and certainly to act joyfully brings joy to others, which in turn makes one feel joyful.

Dorothy Day

May 20

May 21

Nothing can match the treasure of common memories, of trials endured together, of quarrels and reconciliations and generous emotions.

Antoine de Saint-Exupéry

The gift of friendship—both given and received—is joy, love, and nurturing for the heart. The realization that you have met a soul mate...a kindred spirit...a sister...a true friend...is one of life's sweetest gifts!

May 22

May 23

Every good and perfect gift is from above, coming down from the Father of the heavenly lights, who does not change like shifting shadows.

James 1:17 NIV

What a heavenly thing it is;
World without end....
Such friends God has given me.

Celia Thaxter

May 24

May 25

Living the truth in your heart without compromise brings kindness into the world.

18th Century Monk

His tenderness in the springing grass,
His beauty in the flowers,
His living love in the sun above—
All here, and near, and ours.

Charlotte Perkins Gilman

May 26

May 27

A fiery sunset, tiny pansies by the wayside, the sound of raindrops tapping on the roof—what an extraordinary delight to share simple wonders with a true friend! With wide eyes and full hearts, you and I have come to cherish what others have missed.

"For I know the plans I have for you,"
declares the Lord, "plans to prosper you
and not to harm you, plans to give you
hope and a future."

Jeremiah 29:11 NIV

May 28

May 29

When we recall the past, we usually find that it is the simplest things—not the great occasions—that in retrospect give off the greatest glow of happiness.

Bob Hope

Communication means a sharing together
of what you really are. With the stethoscope
of love you listen until you hear the
heartbeat of the other.

Bartlett and Margaret Hess

May 30

May 31

Some of the most rewarding and beautiful moments of a friendship happen in the unforeseen open spaces between planned activities. It is important that you allow these spaces to exist.

Christine Leefeldt

When you are truly joined in spirit,
another woman's good is your good too. You
work for the good of each other.

Ruth Senter

June 1

June 2

Before God made us, He loved us.... And in this love our life is everlasting.

Julian of Norwich

Beloved, since God loved us so much, we also ought to love one another.

1 John 4:11 NRSV

$\mathcal{S}$eeing how God works in nature can help us understand how He works in our lives.

Janette Oke

$\mathcal{J}$une 3

June 4

Friendship is based upon
What we give, not what we take,
And it steers its kindly course
For a special friend's own sake.

Edith H. Shank

$\mathcal{S}$ome people come into our lives and quickly go. Some stay for a while and leave footprints on our hearts and we are never, ever the same.

$\mathcal{J}$une 5

June 6

"Just living is not enough," said the butterfly. "One must have sunshine, freedom, and a little flower."

Hans Christian Andersen

$\mathcal{B}$e kind to one another, tenderhearted, forgiving one another, as God in Christ has forgiven you.

Ephesians 4:32 NRSV

$\mathcal{J}$une 7

June 8

Friendship is not diminished by distance or time...by suffering or silence. It is in these things that it roots most deeply. It is from these things that it flowers.

$\mathcal{M}$ost new discoveries are suddenly-seen
things that were always there.

Susanne K. LANGER

$\mathcal{J}$une 9

June 10

Live for today but hold your hands open to tomorrow. Anticipate the future and its changes with joy. There is a seed of God's love in every event, every circumstance, every unpleasant situation in which you may find yourself.

Barbara Johnson

Summer afternoon—summer aftenoon;
to me those have always been the two most
beautiful words in the English language.

Henry James

June 11

June 12

Listen to your life. See it for the fathomless mystery that it is. In the boredom and pain of it no less than in the excitement and gladness: touch, taste, smell your way to the holy and hidden heart of it because in the last analysis all moments are key moments and life itself is grace.

Frederich Buechner

The Lord will guide you always;
He will satisfy your needs....
You will be like a well-watered garden,
like a spring whose waters never fail.

Isaiah 58:11 NIV

June 13

June 14

God loves and cares for us, even to the least event and smallest need of life.

Henry Edward Manning

$\mathcal{B}$less God for the love of friends so true,
A love akin to His,
Which knows our faults and loves us still;
That's what real friendship is.

Pat Lassen

$\mathcal{J}une\ 15$

June 16

We have been in God's thought from all eternity, and in His creative love, His attention never leaves us.

Michael Quoist

There is no duty we so much underrate
as the duty of being happy. By being happy
we sow anonymous benefits upon the world.

Robert Louis Stevenson

June 17

June 18

As far as God is concerned, there is a sweet, wholesome fragrance in our lives. It is the fragrance of Christ within us.

2 Corinthians 2:15 TLB

Fame is the scentless sunflower,
with gaudy crown of gold;
But friendship is the breathing rose,
with sweets in every fold.

Oliver Wendell Holmes

June 19

June 20

Our Creator would never have made such lovely days, and given us the deep hearts to enjoy them, above and beyond all thought, unless we were meant to be immortal.

Nathaniel Hawthorne

From quiet homes and
first beginning
Out to the undiscovered ends.
There's nothing worth the wear of winning,
But laughter and the love of friends.

Hilaire Belloc

June 21

June 22

How sweet the sound of friends laughing together, of sharing the joy of knowing each other so well.

May your hours of reminiscence be filled with days of good cheer and weeks of pleasant memories.

May the God of hope fill you with all joy and peace as you trust in him.

Romans 15:13 NIV

June 23

June 24

What made us friends in the long ago
When we first met?
Well, I think I know;
The best in me and the best in you
Hailed each other because they knew
That always and always since life began
Our being friends was part of God's plan.

George Webster Douglas

$\mathcal{A}$ smile costs nothing but gives much. It takes but a moment, but the memory of it sometimes lasts forever.

$\mathcal{J}$une 25

June 26

Heaven comes down to touch us when we find ourselves safe in the heart of another.

Having someone who understands is
a great blessing for ourselves. Being someone
who understands is a great blessing to others.

Janette Oke

June 27

June 28

If we walk in the light, as he is in the light,
we have fellowship with one another.

1 John 1:7 NIV

Life is what we are alive to. It is not length but breadth.... Be alive to...goodness, kindness, purity, love, history, poetry, music, flowers, stars, God, and eternal hope.

Maltbie D. Babcock

June 29

June 30

The miracles of nature do not seem miracles because they are so common. If no one had ever seen a flower, even a dandelion would be the most startling event in the world.

If we had all the riches
that we could ever spend,
it could never buy the treasures
the heart finds in a friend.

July 1

July 2

A kind heart is a fountain of gladness,
making everything in its vicinity
freshen into smiles.

Washington Irving

The breath of divine love clothes
us in beauty.

For God is sheer beauty,
all generous in love,
loyal always and ever.

Psalm 100:5 THE MESSAGE

July 3

July 4

The ordinary acts we practice every day at home are of more importance to the soul than their simplicity might suggest.

Sir Thomas More

To discover a kindred spirit is to find your
heart in the heart of a friend.

Ann D. Parrish

July 5

July 6

God makes our lives a medley of joy
and tears, hope and help, love
and encouragement.

$\mathcal{T}$here is nothing better than the encouragement of a good friend.

Katherine Butler Hathaway

$\mathcal{J}uly$ 7

July 8

Let [God] have all your worries and cares,
for he is always thinking about you and
watching everything that concerns you.

1 Peter 5:7 TLB

We do not understand the intricate pattern of the stars in their courses, but we know that He who created them does, and that just as surely as He guides them, He is charting a safe course for us.

Billy Graham

July 9

July 10

Night jasmine blooming brings
memories flooding through my mind
of a screened-in porch at twilight,
the quiet hum of a ceiling fan,
the squeak of a white-wicker rocker,
an icy glass of lemonade,
intimate conversation with a treasured friend,
and time...time just to be.

Line by line, moment by moment,
special times are etched into our memories
in the permanent ink of everlasting love
in our relationships.

Gloria Gaither

July 11

July 12

Meeting someone for the first time is like going on a treasure hunt. What wonderful worlds we can find in others!

Edward E. Ford

Let us outdo each other in being helpful and kind to each other and in doing good.

Hebrews 10:24 TLB

July 13

July 14

Friends that hold each other accountable usually have a deep, abiding, and open relationship.... Being aware that a friend cares enough to make us accountable creates a stronger bond.

If you can learn to laugh in spite of the circumstances that surround you, you will enrich others, enrich yourself, and more than that, you will last!

Barbara Johnson

July 15

July 16

Through the eyes of our friends, we learn to see ourselves...through the love of our friends, we learn to love ourselves...through the caring of our friends, we learn what it means to be ourselves completely.

$\mathcal{J}$ust as there comes a warm sunbeam into every cottage window, so comes a love—born of God's care for every separate need.

Nathaniel Hawthorne

$\mathcal{J}$uly 17

July 18

You are a blessing
sent from Heaven above,
a huggable reminder
of God's unfailing love.

God is love. Whoever lives in love lives in God,
and God in him.

1 John 4:16 NIV

There are no little things. "Little things,"
so called, are the hinges of the universe.

Fanny Fern

July 19

Something deep in all of us yearns for God's beauty, and we can find it no matter where we are.

Sue Monk Kidd

Love is not getting, but giving.... It is goodness and honor and peace and pure living—yes, love is that and it is the best thing in the world and the thing that lives the longest.

Henry Van Dyke

July 21

July 22

Everyone was meant to share
God's all-abiding love and care;
He saw that we would need to know
a way to let these feelings show....
So God made hugs.

Jill Wolf

When others are happy, be happy with them. If they are sad, share their sorrow.

Romans 12:15 TLB

July 23

July 24

When I recollect the treasure of friendship that has been bestowed upon me, I withdraw all charges against life. If much has been denied me, much, very much has been given me. So long as the memory of certain beloved friends lives in my heart, I shall say that life is good.

Helen Keller

Reverie is not a mind vacuum. It is rather the gift of an hour which knows the plenitude of the soul.

Gaston Bachelard

July 25

July 26

Those who sow courtesy reap friendship,
and those who plant kindness gather love.

Hold fast your dreams!
Within you heart
Keep one still, secret spot
Where dreams may go
And, sheltered so,
May thrive and grow.

Louise Driscoll

July 27

July 28

The Lord your God is with you....
He will take great delight in you,
he will quiet you with his love,
he will rejoice over you with singing.

Zephaniah 3:17 NIV

I'd like to be the sort of friend
that you have been to me.
I'd like to be the help that you've
been always glad to be;
I'd like to mean as much to you
each minute of the day
As you have meant, old friend of mine,
to me along the way.

Edgar A. Guest

July 29

July 30

If I could reach up and hold a star for every time you've made me smile, the entire evening sky would be in the palm of my hand.

$\mathcal{L}$ove in the heart wasn't put there to stay;
love isn't love 'til you give it away.

Oscar Hammerstein II

$\mathcal{J}$uly 31

August 1

The glory of friendship is found in the inspiration that comes when I discover that someone else believes in me and is willing to trust me with their friendship.

Embrace this God-life. Really embrace
it, and nothing will be too much for you....
That's why I urge you to pray for absolutely
everything, ranging from small to large.
Include everything as you embrace this
God-life, and you'll get God's everything.

Mark 11:22-24 THE MESSAGE

August 2

August 3

May you always find three
welcomes in life,
In a garden during summer,
At a fireside during winter,
And whatever the day or season
In the kind eyes of a friend.

Some days, it is enough encouragement just to watch the clouds break up and disappear, leaving behind a blue patch of sky and bright sunshine that is so warm upon my face. It's a glimpse of divinity; a kiss from heaven.

August 4

August 5

We have not made ourselves; we are the gift of the living God to one another.

Reine Duell Bethany

My friend is not perfect—no more than
I am—and so we suit each other admirably.

Alexander Smith

August 6

August 7

Thank you for your laughter, warm smile, and ever-present love that so often lifts me up above the clouds to where the sun is always shining.

Two are better than one...for if they fall, one will lift up the other.

Ecclesiastes 4:9-10 NRSV

$\mathcal{A}$ beautiful woman appeals to the eye;
a good woman appeals to the heart.
One is a jewel; the other, a treasure.

Napoleon Bonaparte

$\mathcal{A}$ugust 8

August 9

See each morning a world made anew, as if it were the morning of the very first day;...treasure and use it, as if it were the final hour of the very last day.

Fay Hartzell Arnold

There is nothing on this earth more to be prized than true friendship.

Thomas Aquinas

August 10

August 11

If I were to make a solemn speech in praise
of you, in gratitude, in deep affection,
you would turn an alarming shade of
crimson and try to escape. So I won't.
Take it all as said.

Marion Garretty

Love is little deeds we show,
Love will make my spirit grow;
Grow in peace, grow in light
Love will do the thing that's right.

Charles Dalmon

Love...keeps no record of wrongs.

1 Corinthians 13:4-5 NIV

August 12

August 13

All that we have and are is one of the unique and never-to-be-repeated ways God has chosen to express Himself in space and time. Each of us, made in His image and likeness, is yet another promise He has made to the universe that He will continue to love it and care for it.

Brennan Manning

Friendships begun in this world can be taken up again in heaven, never to be broken off.

Francis de Sales

August 14

August 15

For attractive lips,
Speak words of kindness.
For lovely eyes,
Seek out the good in people.
For a slim figure,
Share your food with the hungry.
For beautiful hair,
Let a child run his or her fingers
through it once a day.
For poise,
Walk with the knowledge you'll
never walk alone.

Audrey Hepburn

$\mathcal{G}$od's heart is the most sensitive and tender of all. No act goes unnoticed, no matter how insignificant or small.

Richard J. Foster

$\mathcal{A}$ugust 16

August 17

You will go out in joy
and be led forth in peace;
the mountains and hills
will burst into song before you,
and all the trees of the field
will clap their hands.

Isaiah 55:12 NIV

$\mathcal{P}$eople who have warm friends are
healthier and happier.... A single real friend
is a treasure worth more than
gold or precious stones.

C. D. Prentice

$\mathcal{A}$ugust 18

August 19

There is something very powerful about...someone believing in you, someone giving you another chance.

Sheila Walsh

Hearts never lose touch; friendships
linger forever in a place that no words
could ever describe.

August 20

August 21

Do a deed of simple kindness;
Though its end you may not see,
It may reach, like widening ripples,
Down a long eternity.

Joseph Norris

I remember the times you were there for me, showing real interest and concern. I'm thankful for the closeness we share. How I enjoy being with you!

A friend loves at all times.

Proverbs 17:17 NIV

August 22

August 23

Few delights can equal the mere presence
of one whom we trust utterly.

George MacDonald

$\mathcal{G}$o outside, to the fields, enjoy nature
and the sunshine, go out and try to recapture
happiness in yourself and in God.
Think of all the beauty that's still left in and
around you and be happy!

Anne Frank

$\mathcal{A}$ugust 24

August 25

We need both...the joy of the sense
of sound; and the equally great joy
of its absence.

Madeleine L'Engle

When our friends are present we ought to treat them well: and when they are absent, to speak of them well.

Epictetus

August 26

August 27

If I had a single flower for every time I think
about you, I could walk forever
in my garden.

*I thank my God upon every
remembrance of you.*

Philippians 1:3 KJV

May the hand of a friend always
be near you;
May God fill your heart with gladness
to cheer you.

Irish Blessing

August 28

August 29

Joys come from simple and natural things:
mists over meadows, sunlight on leaves, the
path of the moon over the water.

Sigurd F. Olson

$\mathcal{G}$od give me joy in the love of friends,
In the dear home talk as summer ends....
In the thought that life has love to spend,
In the faith that God's at journey's end.
God give me hope for each day that springs,
God give me joy in the common things!

Thomas Curtis Clark

$\mathcal{A}$ugust 30

August 31

Laughing at ourselves as well as with each other gives a surprising sense of togetherness.

Hazel C. Lee

May the Lord bless and protect you; may the Lord's face radiate with joy because of you; may he be gracious to you, show you his favor, and give you his peace.

Numbers 6:24-26 TLB

September 1

September 2

Knowing what to say is not always necessary; just the presence of a caring friend can make a world of difference.

Sheri Curry

To speak gratitude is courteous and pleasant, to enact gratitude is generous and noble, but to live gratitude is to touch Heaven.

Johannes A. Gaertner

September 3

September 4

A friend is one who believes in you before you believe in yourself.

Sarah Orne Jewett

To be grateful is to recognize the love of God in everything He has given us—and He has given us everything. Every breath we draw is a gift of His love, every moment of existence a gift of grace.

Thomas Merton

September 5

September 6

This is the day the Lord has made. We will rejoice and be glad in it.

Psalm 118:24 TLB

The day is done, the sun has set,
Yet light still tints the sky;
My heart stands still in reverence,
For God is passing by.

Ruth Alla Wager

September 7

September 8

Thank you for the treasure of your friendship...for showing me God's special heart of love.

Grace and gratitude belong together like heaven and earth. Grace evokes gratitude like the voice an echo. Gratitude follows grace as thunder follows lightning.

Karl Barth

September 9

September 10

Little kindnesses, little acts of
considerateness, little appreciations,
little confidences...they are all that are needed
to keep the friendship sweet.

Hugh Black

$\mathcal{N}$o one has greater love than this, to lay down one's life for one's friends.

John 15:13 NRSV

$\mathcal{S}$eptember 11

September 12

Happy times and bygone days are never lost.... In truth, they grow more wonderful within the heart that keeps them.

Kay Andrew

Friendship is like love at its best: not blind but sympathetically all-seeing; a support which does not wait for understanding; an act of faith which does not need, but always has, reason.

Louis Untermeyer

September 13

September 14

When we dream alone, it remains only a dream. When we dream together, it is not just a dream. It is the beginning of reality.

Dom Helder Camara

$\mathcal{J}$oyfulness keeps the heart and face young. A good laugh makes us better friends with ourselves and everybody around us.

Orison Swett Marden

$\mathcal{S}$eptember 15

September 16

How kind he is! How good he is. So
merciful, this God of ours. The Lord protects
the simple and the childlike.

Psalm 116:5-6 TLB

$\mathcal{B}$egin today! No matter how feeble the light, let it shine as best it may. The world may need just that quality of light which you have.

Henry C. Blinn

$\mathcal{S}$eptember 17

September 18

Life is fortified by many friendships. To love, and to be loved, is the greatest happiness of existence.

Sydney Smith

Friendships, family ties, the companionship of little children...the intricate design and haunting fragrance of a flower...the fluted note of bird song, the glowing glory of a sunset: the world is aflame with things of eternal moment.

E. Margaret Clarkson

September 19

September 20

The real secret of happiness is not what you give or what you receive; it's what you share.

Perfume and incense bring
joy to the heart,
and the pleasantness of one's friend springs
from his earnest counsel.

Proverbs 27:9 NIV

September 21

September 22

From the simple seeds of understanding,
we reap the lovely harvest of true friendship.

$\mathcal{S}$ilences make the real conversations between friends. Not the saying but the never needing to say is what counts.

Margaret Lee Runbeck

$\mathcal{S}$eptember 23

September 24

Where the soul is full of peace and joy,
outward surroundings and circumstances are
of comparatively little account.

Hannah Whitall Smith

How many, many friendships
Life's path has let me see;
I've kept a scrap of each of them
To make the whole of me.

June Masters Bacher

September 25

September 26

May the Lord keep watch between you
and me when we are away from each other.

Genesis 31:49 NIV

Who we are is connected to those we love and to those who have influenced us toward goodness.

Christopher de Vinck

September 27

September 28

What is important is that one is capable
of love. It is perhaps the only glimpse
we are permitted of eternity.

Helen Hayes

Kind words are jewels that live in the heart and soul and remain as blessed memories years after they have been spoken.

Marvea Johnson

September 29

September 30

Friendship is the fruit gathered from the trees planted in the rich soil of love, and nurtured with tender care and understanding.

Alma L. Weixelbaum

The steadfast love of the Lord is from
everlasting to everlasting.

Psalm 103:17 NRSV

October 1

October 2

Friendship...is indeed genuine when two friends, without speaking a word to each other, can nevertheless find happiness in being together.

George Ebers

*T*ake a risk. Open up your heart. Find a
real friend and grow together. Be a real friend
and see what happens.

Sheila Walsh

*O*ctober 3

October 4

One taper lights a thousand,
Yet shines as it has shone;
And the humblest light may kindle
A brighter than its own.

Hezekian Butterworth

$\mathcal{O}$f all best things upon the earth, I hold that a faithful friend is the best.

EDWARD BULWER-LYTTON

October 6

Kind words are the music of the world.

Frederick W. Faber

Live in harmony and peace.
And may the God of love and peace
be with you.

2 Corinthians 13:11 TLB

Joy is warm and radiant and clamors for expressions and experience.

Dorothy Segovia

October 7

October 8

The best friendships have weathered misunderstandings and trying times. One of the secrets of a good relationship is the ability to accept the storms.

Alan Loy McGinnis

$\mathcal{G}$etting things accomplished isn't nearly
as important as taking time for love.

Janette Oke

$\mathcal{O}$ctober 9

October 10

Love is the seed of all hope. It is the enticement to trust, to risk, to try, to go on.

Gloria Gaither

$\mathcal{D}$ear friends, let us practice loving each other, for love comes from God and those who are loving and kind show that they are the children of God.

I John 4:7 TLB

$\mathcal{O}$ctober 11

October 12

I am beginning to learn that it is the sweet, simple things of life which are the real ones after all.

Laura Ingalls Wilder

Love makes burdens lighter, because you divide them. It makes joys more intense, because you share them. It makes you stronger, so that you can reach out and become involved with life in ways you dared not risk alone.

October 13

October 14

Far away, there in the sunshine, are my
highest aspirations.... I can look up and see
their beauty, believe in them, and try to
follow where they lead.

Louisa May Alcott

Thank you, Lord, for the grace of your love,
for the grace of friendship, and for
the grace of beauty.

Henri J. M. Nouwen

October 16

Love is very patient and kind.... If you love someone...you will always believe in him, always expect the best of him, and always stand your ground in defending him.

1 Corinthians 13:4,7 TLB

I asked God for all things that I might enjoy life. He gave me life that I might enjoy all things.

October 17

October 18

As the ocean is never full of water,
so is the heart never full of love.

The best things are nearest: breath in your nostrils, light in your eyes, flowers at your feet, duties at your hand, the path of God just before you.

Robert Louis Stevenson

October 19

October 20

My heart is content with just knowing
Fulfillment that true friendship brings;
It fills to the brim, overflowing
With pleasure in life's "little things."

June Masters Bacher

$\mathcal{Y}$ou're my place of quiet retreat;
I wait for your Word to renew me....
Therefore I lovingly embrace
everything you say.

Psalm 119:114,119 THE MESSAGE

$\mathcal{O}$ctober 21

October 22

A friend is one who joyfully sings with you when you are on the mountain top, and silently walks beside you through the valley.

William A. Ward

Happiness is excitement that has found a settling down place, but there is always a little corner that keeps flapping around.

E. L. Konigsburg

October 23

October 24

A good friend will sharpen your character, draw your soul into the light, and challenge your heart to love in a greater way.

Love is always bestowed as a gift—freely, willingly, and without expectation.... We don't love to be loved; we love to love.

Leo F. Buscgalia

October 26

May the Lord be loyal to you...and reward you with many demonstrations of his love!

2 Samuel 2:6 TLB

There's happiness in little things,
There's joy in passing pleasure;
But friendships are, from year to year,
The best of all life's treasure.

October 27

October 28

Love is a promise that is always kept, a fortune that can never be spent, a seed that can flourish in even the most unlikely of places. And this radiance that never fades, this mysterious and magical joy, is the greatest treasure of all—one known only by those who love.

The best and most beautiful things in the world cannot be seen or even touched. They must be felt with the heart.

Helen Keller

October 30

A friend is one who says, I've time,
When others have to rush.

June Masters Bacher

$\mathcal{A}$ generous man will prosper;
he who refreshes others will
himself be refreshed.

Proverbs 11:25 NIV

$\mathcal{O}$ctober 31

November 1

I especially value the friends who love me as God loves me—through no merit of my own!

Sharon M. Mason

Whole hearted, ready laughter heals, encourages, relaxes anyone within hearing distance. The laughter that springs from love makes wide the space around—gives room for the loved one to enter in.

Eugenia Price

November 2

November 3

We must know that we have been created for greater things, not just to be a number in the world.... We have been created in order to love and to be loved.

Mother Teresa

It is an extraordinary and beautiful thing that God, in creation...works with the beauty of matter; the reality of things; the discoveries of the senses, all five of them; so that we, in turn, may hear the grass growing; see a face springing to life in love and laughter.... The offerings of creation...our glimpses of truth.

Madeleine L'Engle

November 4

November 5

Dear friend, I pray that you may enjoy good health and that all may go well with you.

3 John 1:2 NIV

Into all our lives, in many simple, familiar, homely ways, God infuses this element of joy from the surprises of life, which unexpectedly brighten our days, and fill our eyes with light.

Longfellow

November 6

November 7

The beauty of the earth, the beauty of the sky, the order of the stars, the sun, the moon...their very loveliness is their confession of God.

Augustine

Friends remind us we are part of
something greater than ourselves,
a larger world.

Barbara Jenkins

November 8

November 9

The beauty of a woman is not in
the clothes she wears,
The figure that she carries, or the
way she combs her hair.
The beauty of a woman must be seen
from in her eyes,
Because that is the doorway to her heart,
the place where love resides.

Audrey Hepburn

Oh, give thanks to the Lord, for he is so good! For his loving-kindness is forever.

Psalm 118:29 TLB

November 10

November 11

Loving and being loved is the greatest of human joys, the ultimate human experience. We can exist without love; but we are not living fully as human beings without it.

Edward E. Ford

Can you measure the value
of friendship,
Of knowing that someone is there,
Of faith and of hope and of courage,
A treasured and goodly share?

Garnett Ann

November 12

November 13

God created us with an overwhelming desire to soar.... He designed us to be tremendously productive and "to mount up with wings like eagles," realistically dreaming of what He can do with our potential.

Carol Kent

We all mold one another's dreams. We all hold each other's fragile hopes in our hands. We all touch others' hearts.

November 14

November 15

I thank God far more for friends than for my daily bread—for friendship is the bread of the heart.

Mary Mitford

I have not stopped giving thanks for you, remembering you in my prayers.

Ephesians 1:16 NIV

To know someone here or there with whom you feel there is an understanding in spite of distances or thoughts unexpressed—that can make of this earth a garden.

Goethe

November 16

November 17

If we learn how to give of ourselves, to forgive others, and to live with thanksgiving, we need not seek happiness. It will seek us.

I f you surrender completely to the moments as they pass, you live more richly those moments.

Anne Morrow Lindbergh

November 18

November 19

Friendship: It involves many things, but above all, the power of going out of one's self and seeing and appreciating whatever is noble and loving in another.

Thomas Hughes

There is always a time for gratitude and new beginnings.

J. Robert Moskin

In everything give thanks.

1 Thessalonians 5:18 KJV

November 20

November 21

Sooner or later we begin to understand...that love is here and now, real and true, the most important thing in our lives. For love is the creator of our favorite memories and the foundation of our fondest dreams.

$\mathcal{C}$herish your human connections: your relationships with friends and family.

Barbara Bush

$\mathcal{N}$ovember 22

November 23

Of all the heavenly gifts
that mortal men commend,
What trusty treasure in the world
can countervail a friend?

Nicholas Grimald

$\mathcal{T}$here is something in every season, in
every day, to celebrate with thanksgiving.

Gloria Gaither

$\mathcal{N}$ovember 24

November 25

A thankful person can find contentment anywhere.

Give thanks to the Lord, for he is good;
his love endures forever.

Psalm 106:1 NIV

$\mathcal{T}$hanksgiving is a time of quiet reflection...an annual reminder that God has, again, been ever so faithful. The solid and simple things of life are brought into clear focus.

Charles Swindoll

$\mathcal{N}$ovember 26

November 27

True gratitude, like true love, must find expression in acts, not words.

R. Mildred Barker

Friends...they cherish each other's hopes.
They are kind to each other's dreams.

Henry David Thoreau

November 28

November 29

Time is a very precious gift of God; so
precious that it's only given to us
moment by moment.

Amelia Barr

$\mathcal{G}$ratitude is the inward feeling of kindness received. Thankfulness is the natural impulse to express that feeling. Thanksgiving is the following of that impulse.

Henry Van Dyke

$\mathcal{N}$ovember 30

December 1

How silently,
How silently the wondrous gift is given.
So God imparts to human hearts
The wonders of His heaven.

Phillips Brooks

In quietness and trust is your strength.

Isaiah 30:15 NIV

$\mathcal{D}$ear friends, no matter how we find
them, are as essential to our lives as breathing
in and breathing out.

Lois Wyse

$\mathcal{D}$ecember 2

December 3

The first fall of snow is not only an event but it is a magical event. You go to bed in one kind of world and wake up to find yourself in another quite different, and if this is not enchantment, then where is it to be found?

J. B. Priestley

$\mathcal{B}$lessed are those who can give without remembering, and take without forgetting.

Elizabeth Bibesco

$\mathcal{D}$ecember 4

December 5

Happiness is intrinsic, it's an internal thing. When you build it into yourself, no external circumstances can take it away.

Leo Buscaglia

Kindness opens in each heart a little heaven. Dress in the wardrobe God picked out for you: compassion, kindness, humility, quiet strength, discipline.

Colossians 3:12 THE MESSAGE

December 6

December 7

Friendship cheers like a sunbeam; charms like a good story; inspires like a brave leader; binds like a golden chain; guides like a heavenly vision.

Newell Dwight Hillis

I believe that we are always attracted to what we need most, an instinct leading us toward the persons who are to open new vistas in our lives and fill them with new knowledge.

Helene Iswolski

December 8

December 9

Our road will be smooth and
untroubled no matter what care
life may send;
If we travel the pathway together,
and walk side by side with a friend.

Henry Van Dyke

It is good and pleasant
when God's people live together in peace!

Psalm 133:1 NCV

December 10

December 11

I value the friend who for me finds time on [her] calendar, but I cherish the friend who for me does not consult the calendar.

Robert Brault

The things that matter the most in this world, they can never be held in our hand.

Gloria Gaither

December 12

December 13

We expect too much at Christmas. It's got to be magical. It's got to go right. Feasting. Fun. The perfect present. All that anticipation. Take it easy. Love's the thing. The rest is tinsel.

Pam Brown

$\mathcal{M}$ay no gift be too small to give,
nor too simple to receive,
which is wrapped in thoughtfulness
and tied with love.

L. O. Baird

$\mathcal{D}$ecember 14

December 15

May the Lord of peace himself give you
peace at all times and in every way.

2 Thessalonians 3:16 NIV

Happiness is being at peace, being with loved ones, being comfortable. But most of all, it's having those loved ones.

Johnny Cash

December 16

December 17

A friend is someone who understands
your past, believes in your future, and accepts
you today just the way you are.

Beverly LaHaye

God's peace is joy resting.
His joy is peace dancing.

F. F. Bruce

December 18

December 19

How will you your Christmas keep?
Feasting, fasting, or asleep?...
Be it kept with joy or pray'r,
Keep of either some to spare;
Whatsoever brings the day,
Do not keep but give away.

Eleanor Farjeon

$\mathcal{B}$ehold, a virgin shall be with child, and shall bring forth a son, and they shall call his name Emmanuel, which being interpreted is, God with us.

Matthew 1:23 KJV

$\mathcal{D}$ecember 20

December 21

Trust your friends with both the delightful and the difficult parts of your life.

Luci Shaw

For somehow, not only at Christmas, but all the long year through, the joy that you give to others is the joy that comes back to you.

John Greenleaf Whittier

December 22

December 23

The most vivid memories of Christmases past are usually not of gifts given or received, but of the spirit of love, the special warmth of Christmas worship, the cherished little habits of the home, the results of others acting in the spirit of Christ.

Lois Rand

$\mathcal{G}$od grant you the light in Christmas,
which is faith; the warmth of Christmas,
which is love...the all of Christmas,
which is Christ.

Wilda English

$\mathcal{D}$ecember 24

December 25

For to us a child is born,
to us a son is given,
and the government will be on his shoulders.
And he will be called
Wonderful Counselor, Mighty God,
Everlasting Father, Prince of Peace.

Isaiah 9:6 NIV

Many merry Christmases, many happy New Years. Unbroken friendships, great accumulations of cheerful recollections and affections on earth, and heaven for us all.

Charles Dickens

December 26

December 27

Still round the corner there may wait,
A new road, or a secret gate.

J. R. R. Tolkien

Down the dark future, through
long generations,
The echoing sounds grow fainter
and then cease;
And like a bell, with solemn, sweet vibrations,
I hear once more the voice of Christ say
"Peace!"

Longfellow

December 28

December 29

The special closeness and understanding that two people so rarely share is part of the magic of our friendship.

Ｇod knows the rhythm of my spirit and knows my heart thoughts. He is as close as breathing.

God takes care of all
who stay close to him.

Psalm 31:23 THE MESSAGE

Ｄecember 30

December 31

The book is closed...
The year is done,
The pages full
Of tasks begun....
And may we find
Before the end,
A deep content...
Another friend.

Arch Ward